CANADIAN RESOURCES

NATURAL GAS

BY THE NUMBERS

Jason McClure

Weigl

Published by Weigl Educational Publishers Limited
6325 10th Street SE
Calgary, Alberta, Canada
T2H 2Z9

Website: www.weigl.ca

Library and Archives Canada Cataloguing in Publication available
upon request. Fax 403-233-7769 for the attention of the Publishing
Records department.

ISBN 978-1-77071-265-2 (hardcover)

ISBN 978-1-77071-266-9 (softcover)

ISBN 978-1-77071-267-6 (multi-user eBook)

Printed in the United States of America in
North Mankato, Minnesota

1 2 3 4 5 6 7 8 9 0 17 16 15 14 13

072013
WEP130613

Weigl acknowledges Getty Images and Alamy as the primary image
suppliers for this title.

Every reasonable effort has been made to trace ownership and to
obtain permission to reprint copyright material. The publishers
would be pleased to have any errors or omissions brought to their
attention so that they may be corrected in subsequent printings.

We acknowledge the financial support of the Government of Canada
through the Canada Book Fund for our publishing activities.

Project Coordinator
Heather Kissock

Art Director
Terry Paulhus

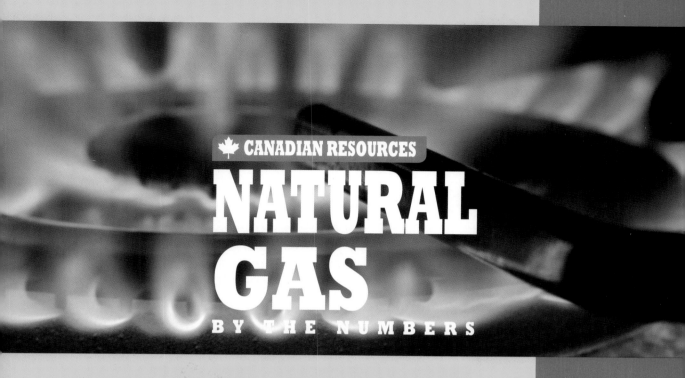

CANADIAN RESOURCES

NATURAL GAS

BY THE NUMBERS

CONTENTS

Large drilling machines are used to dig holes toward the natural gas source.

Natural Gas Resources

"Natural gas is the future. It is here."
Bill Richardson, American politician

Natural gas is one of Canada's key **natural resources**. Found deep underground, people obtain natural gas by drilling holes into the earth. Natural gas is used as fuel. It can power everything from cars to homes. Countries that do not have access to natural gas **reserves** rely on countries that have this resource. Canada makes a significant amount of money selling its natural gas to other countries.

A Long Process

Natural gas is a **fossil fuel**. It took millions of years for it to form.

Plants and animals die and sink to the sea floor.

Layers of dirt and sediment cover the remains.

Heat and pressure turn the remains into fossil fuels, including natural gas.

Where Natural Gas Is Found

As natural gas is made from **organic** material, it is found mainly in areas that once had an abundance of plants and animals. Most of the world's known natural gas reserves are located in Eurasia and the Middle East. However, scientists believe that there are other reserves that have yet to be discovered. Natural gas is a non-renewable resource. This means that it cannot be replaced once it is used. Companies are constantly searching for new reserves to maintain the world's natural gas supply.

Some natural gas reserves have been found deep in the seabed. Offshore drilling platforms help companies access these reserves.

As a whole, the Middle East has the most natural gas reserves. However, individually, the countries that make up the Middle East are no competition for Russia. It is estimated that the oil reserves in this country hold more than 47 billion cubic metres.

Natural Gas in Canada

Natural gas resources can be found across the country. The provinces with the largest reserves have been able to turn the resource into a thriving industry. Alberta is Canada's top producer, at 289 million cubic metres per day. British Columbia ranks behind Alberta, producing 99 million cubic metres per day. Natural gas is also found along Canada's East Coast. While some of these reserves are being accessed, many scientists believe there are other reserves to be found in this area. Reserves in northern Canada also show promise.

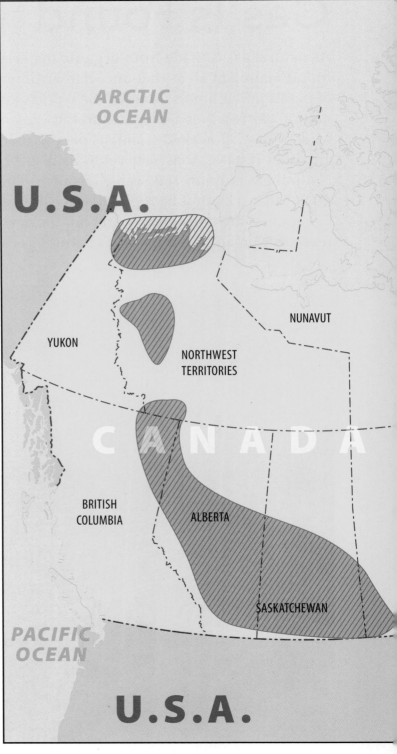

LEGEND	
■	Natural Gas Fields
■	Canada
■	United States and Greenland

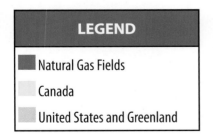

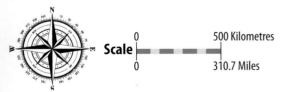

Scale

0 — 500 Kilometres

0 — 310.7 Miles

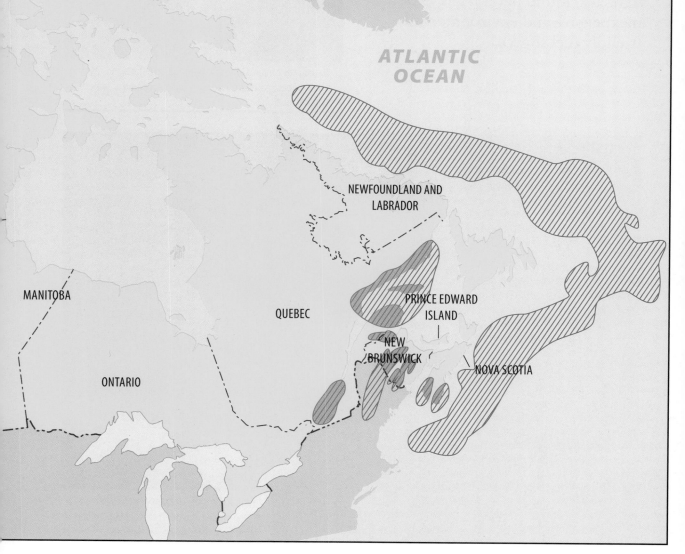

GREENLAND

ATLANTIC
OCEAN

NEWFOUNDLAND AND
LABRADOR

MANITOBA

QUEBEC

PRINCE EDWARD
ISLAND

NEW
BRUNSWICK

ONTARIO

NOVA SCOTIA

Natural Gas Products

As a fuel, natural gas helps to generate power in a number of ways. It is mostly used to heat houses and buildings. However, it can also be used to run equipment and make plastics. Natural gas is used in homes and businesses across the country. Many industries have also found natural gas to be an inexpensive and environmentally friendly fuel source.

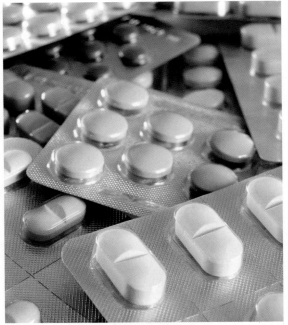

Natural gas contains other gases, including butane and ethane. These gases are used in the manufacturing of some types of medicines.

Natural gas is the cleanest of all fossil fuels. When burned, it produces less pollution than other fossil fuels, such as oil and coal.

Natural Gas at Home

Largely due to the low cost, more and more Canadians are turning to natural gas to heat their homes. They are also finding that natural gas can be used to power household appliances. Many people have gas stoves and gas fireplaces in their homes. Some clothes dryers are run on natural gas. Natural gas can even be used to cool homes. Air conditioners powered by natural gas can be found in many homes.

The Benefits of Natural Gas

Natural gas can power a number of machines and equipment that other fuels are also used to operate. When natural gas is chosen, it can save money and perform better.

Approximately 48 percent of Canadian homes use natural gas for heating. Natural gas costs less than other traditional forms of heating, such as oil.

Natural gas stoves have better temperature control than electric stoves. They can cook food more evenly as well.

Gas fireplaces can supply a constant source of heat. They do not require wood and are turned on and off with a switch.

Natural gas is known to be cleaner than other types of fuels. Cars running on natural gas have fewer **greenhouse gas emissions** than cars running on gasoline and diesel fuels.

Barbecues that are run on natural gas have a constant fuel source. They just have to be turned off and on. Barbecues that run on propane need to have their tanks refilled when they run out of fuel.

From the Ground Up

Getting natural gas from the ground and into homes is a complex process. The gas must be located, and drills have to be set up. Once the gas is at the surface, it has to be cleaned and made ready for use. It is only after all of these steps have taken place that the gas can be sent to homes and businesses.

2

Drilling
Once natural gas is found, drilling machines are set up. They drill into the ground toward the natural gas. When the drill reaches the natural gas, the gas flows to the surface. From here, it travels through a pipeline to a processing plant.

1

Finding the Natural Gas
Scientists use a variety of equipment and methods to search for natural gas underground. They gather information and samples from these methods to decide if the conditions might be present for natural gas to have formed.

Processing

When the natural gas arrives at the processing plant, it is put through a cleaning and separation process. This removes any **impurities** from the natural gas.

Shipping

Once the impurities are removed, the gas is directed into pipelines that move it away from the processing plant toward gas utility companies. At the utility company, a chemical is added to the gas. This chemical gives the gas an odour that allows it to be recognized in case of a leak.

Ready for Use

The gas is now ready to be sent to homes and businesses. It leaves the utility company via a gas main, or underground pipeline. It then travels into the communities the utility company serves. Customers receive the gas through smaller pipes that are connected to their homes and businesses.

In the Neighbourhood

Many businesses throughout Canada rely on natural gas for their heating and cooling needs. Some even use natural gas to provide their lighting. Restaurants often use natural gas ovens to cook their orders.

This is due mainly to the quick flame, which allows for faster cooking times, and the lower cost of natural gas. Natural gas can also be converted into electricity. Businesses that have the proper equipment can use natural gas to power their appliances and machinery.

Restaurants can cook hundreds of meals each day. Using natural gas ovens helps them save money and still deliver well-prepared food.

While most vehicles in Canada still use gasoline for fuel, some cars and trucks are now using natural gas instead. Schoolbuses and city buses are also making the change to natural gas.

Natural Gas in Industry

Industries across the country rely on natural gas as an energy source. As in homes and businesses, industries use natural gas for heating and cooling. However, natural gas can also be used to make certain products. It is a key ingredient in the production of plastics, fertilizers, and fabrics. It also plays an important role in the manufacturing process and can be used to heat metals, melt glass, and treat waste. Canadian industries that commonly use natural gas include pulp and paper mills and oil refineries.

Some welders use equipment powered by natural gas to fuse metal pieces together.

Pulp and paper plants use natural gas to heat the water needed to produce steam. Steam plays an important role in the paper making process.

The Natural Gas Industry

Each day, Canadians use 204 million cubic metres of natural gas. That is enough to fill all the Great Lakes several times over. This makes natural gas very important to the Canadian economy. Natural gas is part of the energy industry, which includes oil and electricity production. Together, the energy industry makes up more than $84 billion of the Canadian economy. Of this number, natural gas contributes about $24 billion. Canada's total economy is worth more than $1.7 trillion.

Global Natural Gas Production

Several countries have more natural gas than Canada, but many of them have not taken major steps to begin accessing their reserves. Canada, on the other hand, has turned natural gas production into an important national industry. It is currently the third highest producer of natural gas in the world, producing approximately 163 billion cubic metres per year.

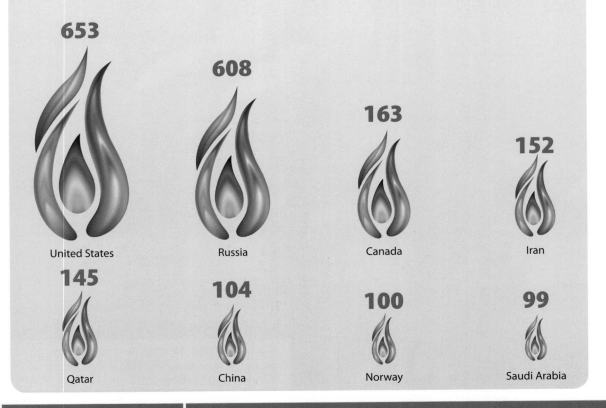

653 — United States
608 — Russia
163 — Canada
152 — Iran
145 — Qatar
104 — China
100 — Norway
99 — Saudi Arabia

Natural Gas Exports

Canada does not use all of its natural gas itself. Most of Canada's natural gas is **exported**. Of all the gas Canada produces, it ships nearly two thirds to the United States. In fact, the United States is the only country Canada ships natural gas to today. Even so, Canada is the fourth largest exporter of natural gas in the world. To get to its destinations, natural gas is pumped through more than 400,000 kilometres of pipelines.

Smaller pipelines connect with major pipelines at various sites along the route. This allows the natural gas to reach customers across the continent.

Global Use of Natural Gas by Region

Each year, global use of natural gas increases about 1.6 percent. North America, especially Canada and the United States, uses the most natural gas, followed by Europe and Eurasia.

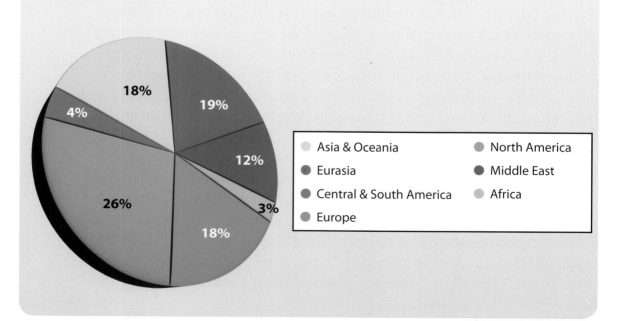

18%
4%
19%
12%
26%
3%
18%

- Asia & Oceania
- Eurasia
- Central & South America
- Europe
- North America
- Middle East
- Africa

Capturing natural gas from decomposing plants will help keep up the supply and make natural gas a renewable resource.

Natural Gas Technology

Canada has two types of natural gas reserves. Conventional natural gas can be easily extracted from underground pools. Unconventional natural gas is more difficult to access. Most of Canada's natural gas reserves are unconventional. As a result, companies have had to develop new technologies to extract it. Canadian companies and individuals have been world leaders in developing these innovations.

Today, a common way of drilling for natural gas is called fracking. Fracking involves breaking up underground rock to get to the natural gas. The process begins with a hole being drilled toward the source of the natural gas. Then, water is mixed with sand and other chemicals and pumped into the hole. The pressure this creates causes the stone to crack or fracture. A substance is then pumped into the cracks to keep them open. This allows the natural gas to escape and flow up the drill hole where it is captured.

Canadian companies are also working on ways to move away from drilling entirely. One area scientists are studying is alternate sources of natural gas. Not all natural gas comes from the ground. As wood and other organic materials break down, they release gas. Companies are working on ways to capture as much of this gas as possible. If they succeed, they will have created **sustainable** natural gas. This type of gas, unlike the natural gas found underground, will never run out. It can be made day after day using regular waste products.

The Process of Fracking

Fracking is considered a fast and cost-effective way to extract natural gas from the ground. However, many people worry about the harm the process causes the environment.

STEP 1
A hole is drilled straight down, or vertically, into the ground.

STEP 2
Drilling begins using a special drill that can move in a horizontal line toward the natural gas source.

STEP 3
Once the source is reached, sand, water, and chemicals are pumped into the hole.

STEP 4
The materials cause enough pressure to break the rocks. Natural gas escapes from the rocks and is pumped up to the surface.

Working with Natural Gas

Natural gas companies also produce oil. Together, the oil and gas industry in Canada employs about 550,000 workers directly and indirectly. Direct jobs are those involved in finding and extracting natural gas and oil. Indirect jobs are created as a result of the industry. They include jobs at gas stations and machine shops. The natural gas industry in Canada is one of the highest paying industries. Each year, natural gas companies pay billions of dollars in salaries.

The Field of Work

The natural gas industry needs a variety of workers to operate. Some are involved in accessing the gas. Others provide the support needed to keep the work flowing.

Engineering

Several types of engineers, including petroleum engineers and chemical engineers, work in the gas industry. These people locate natural gas sources and plan the best ways to access the resource.

Process Workers

Process workers are the people directly involved in getting the natural gas from the ground. Rig workers and production operators belong to this work group.

Support Services

Support workers handle the materials that process workers extract. These workers include truck drivers, inspectors, and general labourers.

Administration

Administrative staff work in the gas company's office. They process the paperwork that helps the company operate and make money. Accountants, receptionists, and executive assistants are all administrative workers.

Natural Gas Jobs

There is a wide range of jobs within the natural gas industry. Each job has different tasks to perform and requires a certain type of training.

Driller

Duties: Operates gas drilling and rig machinery
Education: Secondary school with a college diploma in drilling

Drillers control the equipment that drills a natural gas well. The drillers are the people who actually remove the resource from the ground. Drillers also assist in setting up or taking down drilling rigs, as well as transporting the rigs between sites.

Petroleum Engineer

Duties: Finds methods to improve gas well production
Education: University degree in engineering

Petroleum engineers are responsible for finding new ways to extract natural gas from the ground. They conduct studies for exploration and extraction of the resource. They then plan and supervise projects for the drilling, testing, and reworking of gas wells.

Utilities Manager

Duties: Plans and directs the distribution of natural gas
Education: University degree or college diploma in engineering, business, or another related discipline

Utilities managers are responsible for deciding the rules for providing people with a utility, such as natural gas. They work to make sure that the utility is distributed to the general public at a fair price.

Managing Natural Gas

Natural gas is a valuable resource to many people. However, extracting it from the ground can damage the environment. While processes such as fracking cause problems underground, other damage can occur at the surface. Forests, for example, may need to be removed to build roads, drilling pads, and pipelines. These areas are also home to many plants and animals. They, too, are affected by the development of the land around them.

Governments

Governments set rules that guide how and where natural gas companies can work. These rules tell the companies how large their work site can be and how they must clean any pollution they create. These rules also indicate where drilling is not allowed, such as in protected natural areas.

Individuals

As natural gas is considered a clean fuel, many people are now considering it for their energy needs. People are beginning to use natural gas for more than just heating their homes. However, they are still aware of the environmental effects of extracting the natural gas from the ground. Some people work with environmental groups, governments, and gas companies to ensure that the resource is being extracted in a responsible way.

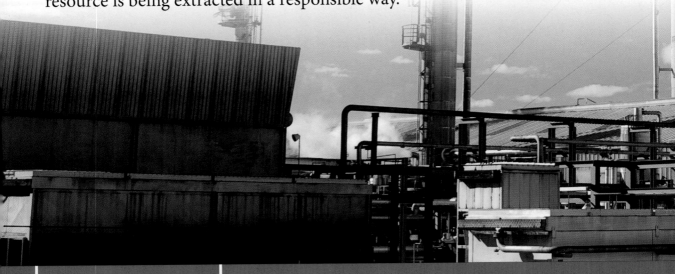

For this reason, natural gas companies must be very careful about where they work. Many different groups, as well as the government, work with oil and gas companies to make sure that Canada's natural gas resources are used properly and that the environment is affected as little as possible.

Companies

Natural gas companies are aware that their work harms the environment. Many companies have programs in place to improve the methods they use to obtain the resource. They hire environmental experts to help them find better ways to access natural gas.

They also look for better and less harmful ways to get natural gas by investing large amounts of money into research.

Environmental Groups

Environmental groups work with governments and gas companies to make sure that the companies are following the rules. These groups also look for land that needs protecting and bring that information to the government and the natural gas companies. They then help develop plans that allow the resource to be accessed with minimal impact to the environment.

Quiz

What type of fuel is natural gas?

A fossil fuel

Which province produces the most natural gas?

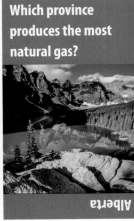

Alberta

How is natural gas shipped to utility companies?

By pipelines

Which continent uses the most natural gas?

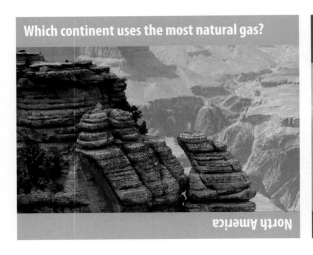

North America

Where does Canada rank in global natural gas production?

Third

What percentage of Canadian homes are heated by natural gas?

About 48 percent

Which country receives all of Canada's natural gas exports?

The United States

What is fracking?

An extraction method that uses water, sand, and chemicals.

Further Resources

Websites to check out!

EcoSpark
www.ecospark.ca/wattwize/students/gas

GazMétro
http://www.allaboutnaturalgas.com/abcs.html

EcoKids
www.ecokids.ca/pub/eco_info/topics/
energy/ecostats/

Activity

Make Natural Gas

Materials Needed: 1 empty 2-litre bottle, 500 millilitres of grass clippings and vegetable scraps, 750 millilitres (1.5 cups) of soil, 1 balloon, duct tape

It may take millions of years for organic material to turn into natural gas, but you can make your own kind of natural gas in just a few days.

1. Mix the grass clippings and vegetable scraps with the soil.
2. Pour the soil mixture into the bottle.
3. Place the end of the balloon over the bottle opening.
4. Secure the balloon to the bottle using the duct tape. It is very important that the balloon is well secured and that there are no small holes or leaks.
5. Place the bottle in a warm place, such as a sunny window, and leave for several days.
6. As the vegetable matter breaks down in the soil, it will begin to release gases, such as methane. This will cause the balloon to begin to inflate. When you are done the experiment, remove the tape and release the gas outside in the fresh air.

Key Words

exported: shipped to another country

fossil fuel: an energy source formed from the remains of plants and animals that lived long ago

greenhouse gas emissions: gases in the air that contribute to global warming

impurities: polluting substances

natural resources: naturally made materials that can be used by people

organic: of or related to living things

reserves: resources known or believed to exist in a certain location

sustainable: able to be maintained at a certain level

Index